How to u... s
Guided Reac...

Walkthrough/Book introduction *(page 2)*

A *walkthrough*, or book introduction, is a way of introducing the book to a group of children. During the walkthrough, children are introduced to some of the ideas and significant vocabulary they will meet when they read the book. The walkthrough for non-fiction books helps you to set up the guided session so that children will know the purpose of the book, how it is made up, and the type of information they can extract from it.

The walkthrough notes on page 2 of this booklet provide prompts for you to use, specific to *From a Bean to a Bar*. Go through the whole of the walkthrough before the children start reading independently. This walkthrough gives you a focus for the book, and the questions, comments and suggestions alert children to the concepts and information they will need in order to read independently and with full understanding.

Independent Reading *(pages 3–5)*

After doing a walkthrough, ask the children to read the text aloud, on their own, at their own pace. Observe the strategies each child uses, praising successful problem solving and expressive reading. Prompts are suggested for good phrasing, use of word-solving skills, predicting and checking the meaning, and actively monitoring the implications of the text.

The Independent Reading notes divide *From a Bean to a Bar* into sections. Look at each section together, then ask the children to read with a particular purpose in mind. These notes provide just one way of tackling an explanation text, so that children can understand the key features of this non-fiction text type.

After Independent Reading/ Returning to the text *(page 6)*

After the children have completed a first reading of the book, return to the text as a group. On page 6, there are quick follow-up ideas for related text, sentence and word level work.

Responding to the text *(pages 6–8)*

It is important to encourage children to give a personal response to the text. Discussion ideas related to the book are given on page 6.

These Teaching Notes also contain group activity ideas on page 7, and a Photocopy Master on page 8, for use after the guided reading session or in a follow-up literacy session.

Guided Reading Notes

Read the title with the children, and ask them what they think the book will tell them. Encourage them to flick through the book very quickly, stressing that they don't have to look closely at every page.

What type of book is it, *fiction* or *non-fiction*? What tells them that it is a non-fiction book?

Title

PROMPTS Find the title and subtitle.

> This book is a non-fiction *report* which *explains* how chocolate is made.

Look at the table of contents and ask children to explain why they think a book about chocolate has sections on trees, pods and beans in it. Ask individual (or pairs of) children to turn to particular sections of the book, e.g. *cutting the pods*, *making chocolate*, and look at the pictures to find out what the information is likely to be about.

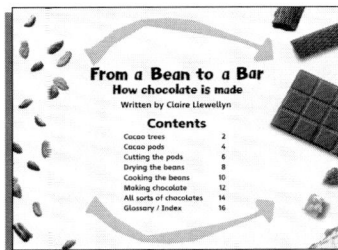

From a Bean to a Bar
How chocolate is made
Written by Claire Llewellyn

Contents

Pages 2–3

PROMPTS Can you find the word *cacao*? Try saying it (say *ka-kow*). Can you find another very similar word on the spread: *cocoa*? *Cacao* is the Spanish word for this tree. We talk about *cacao trees*, *cacao flowers*, and *cacao pods*. From this word we get the English word *cocoa* (say *ko-ko*). We talk about *cocoa beans*, and *cocoa powder*.

Look at the spelling of these two words and try to remember how to spell and pronounce them.

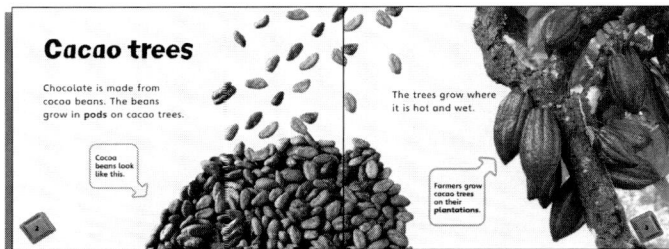

Cacao trees

Chocolate is made from cocoa beans. The beans grow in **pods** on cacao trees.

Cocoa beans look like this.

The trees grow where it is hot and wet.

Farmers grow cacao trees on their plantations.

Explain that you are going to divide the book up into sections: *growing, harvesting* and *what happens at the factory*.

Growing

Look at the pages on *Growing*.

What information can we find out in this part of the book? (*Cacao trees, cacao pods* and *cacao flowers; what chocolate is made from.*) What sort of weather do cacao trees need?

Pages 2–3

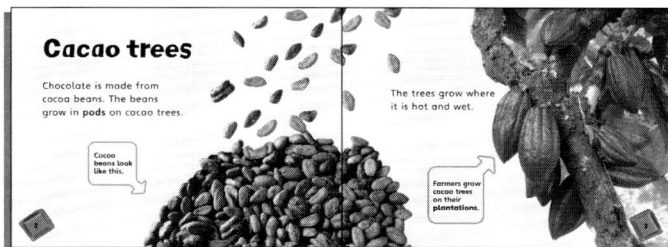

Cacao trees

Chocolate is made from cocoa beans. The beans grow in **pods** on cacao trees.

Cocoa beans look like this.

The trees grow where it is hot and wet.

Farmers grow cacao trees on their **plantations**.

CHECK that the child is using the text and captioned photographs to find information.

CHECK for *cacao*.

"It looks a bit like *cocoa*, doesn't it? Look at the vowel near the beginning."

Pages 4–5

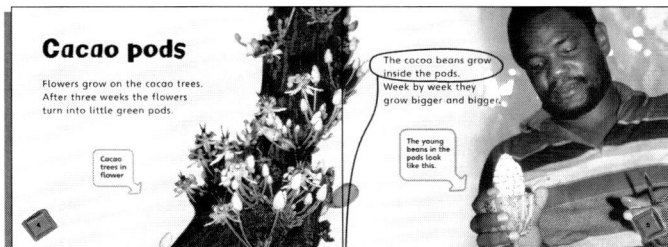

Cacao pods

Flowers grow on the cacao trees. After three weeks the flowers turn into little green pods.

Cacao trees in flower

The cocoa beans grow inside the pods. Week by week they grow bigger and bigger.

The young beans in the pods look like this.

Choose a child to read out the sentence that gives this information.

CHECK that the child picks out the key fact from this spread (*beans grow in pods on cacao trees*).

Harvesting

Ask children to look at the pictures, read the main text and talk about the information in them.

Let's look at these pages on *harvesting* together. Now what is happening to the cacao pods?

Pages 6–7

PROMPTS What colour are the pods now? Why do you think they have changed colour?

What are the people in the pictures doing?

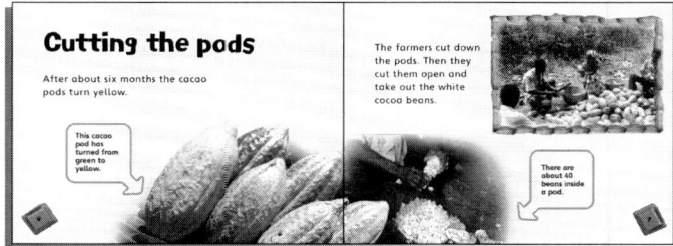

Cutting the pods

After about six months the cacao pods turn yellow.

This cacao pod has turned from green to yellow.

The farmers cut down the pods. Then they cut them open and take out the white cocoa beans.

There are about 40 beans inside a pod.

CHECK that the child reads the heading.

"How do we know this part of the book is about harvesting?"

CHECK that the child reads *cacao* and *cocoa* accurately.

Pages 8–9

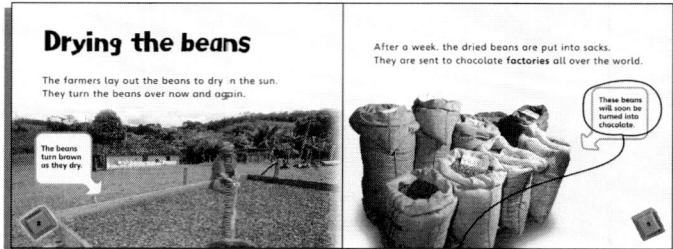

Drying the beans

The farmers lay out the beans to dry in the sun. They turn the beans over now and again.

After a week, the dried beans are put into sacks. They are sent to chocolate **factories** all over the world.

The beans turn brown as they dry.

These beans will soon be turned into chocolate.

Ask individual children to read the captions.

CHECK that the child has picked out the key facts from this spread (*the beans are dried in the sun* and *sent to factories to be processed*).

CHECK that the child understands that **factories** is in bold because it is explained in the glossary.

At the factory

Look at the pages about the factory together.

Where are the cocoa beans now? This section of the book explains what happens when the beans are at the factory.

Page 10–11

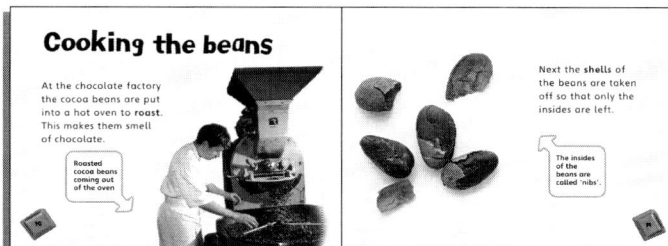

Cooking the beans

At the chocolate factory the cocoa beans are put into a hot oven to **roast**. This makes them smell of chocolate.

Roasted cocoa beans coming out of the oven.

Next the **shells** of the beans are taken off so that only the insides are left.

The insides of the beans are called 'nibs'.

CHECK that the child knows how to use the glossary.

"Can you find a word here that is in bold? Do you know why? Look at the glossary to check the meanings."

Page 12–13

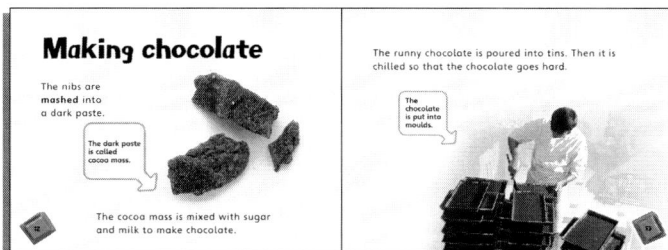

Making chocolate

The nibs are **mashed** into a dark paste.

The dark paste is called cocoa mass.

The cocoa mass is mixed with sugar and milk to make chocolate.

The runny chocolate is poured into tins. Then it is chilled so that the chocolate goes hard.

The chocolate is put into moulds.

CHECK that the child picks up the key facts from this spread.

Glossary: page 16

CHECK that the child uses initial letters to locate words in the glossary.

Turn back to page 10 and ask children to find a word that is in the glossary.

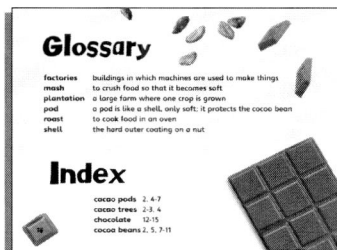

Glossary

factories	buildings in which machines are used to make things
mash	to crush food so that it becomes soft
plantation	a large farm where one crop is grown
pod	a pod is like a shell, only soft; it protects the cocoa bean
roast	to cook food in an oven
shell	the hard outer coating on a nut

Index

cocoa pods	2, 4-7
cocoa trees	2-3, 4
chocolate	12-15
cocoa beans	2, 5, 7-11

Summary

Discuss what the children have found out from the book. Were they right about the sort of information it contained? Does it explain clearly how chocolate is made?

After Independent Reading/Returning to the text

Word knowledge – discriminate syllables

As a group, clap out the syllables of the following words: *chocolate, flowers, inside, factory, oven, runny, sometimes.* Decide which have two syllables and which have three.

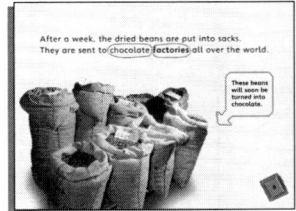

Sentence knowledge – identify words and phrases that link sentences

Ask children to pick out words that help to explain what happens when, e.g. *after, then, next.*

Text knowledge – understand the purpose of an explanation text

Ask the children to run through the process of making chocolate. Encourage them to use the book to help them remember what happens when, and to think about why the book is divided into 3 different sections.

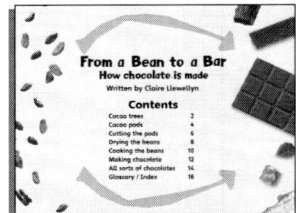

Responding to the text

- How long do the children think it takes for the cacao pods to grow and turn yellow?
- What makes the beans smell of chocolate?
- Did the children find out anything new about chocolate?
- Which part of the book did they find most interesting?

① How chocolate is made

AIM to make a flowchart that explains how chocolate is made
(*NLS: Y2 T2 T21*)

YOU WILL NEED
- flip chart or whiteboard
- simple flowchart diagram, either pre-drawn or drawn as you go along
- coloured pens

WHAT TO DO Remind the children of how they 'chunked' the book about how chocolate is made during the guided reading session (*growing, harvesting, at the factory*). Scan these sections and ask the children to summarize what happens in each one, e.g.
> growing
> beans grow in pods on cacao trees
> farmers cut down the pods, etc.

Write their suggestions on the flipchart and then work as a group to put them in the correct order. Ask the children to suggest headings for each section of the chart.

② Make a 'chocolate' dictionary

AIM to find out the meaning of unfamiliar words; to use dictionaries and glossaries (*NLS: Y2 T2 W10; T16*)

YOU WILL NEED
- selection of dictionaries
- paper and pens/pencils

WHAT TO DO Tell the children to scan the text and list 6 words which are unfamiliar to them. Talk about how we use glossaries and dictionaries to locate words using the initial letter. Children can then refer to the glossary (on page 16 of the book) or look in a dictionary to find out the meaning of the words in their list. They can share their definitions with other children in the group or with the rest of the class during the plenary. This can then be developed in to a class 'chocolate' dictionary.

Making shortbread

These instructions are all jumbled up!
Can you put them in the right order?

Roll the ball out until it is biscuit thin.

Mix the flour and sugar, then rub in the butter.

Squeeze it all together until it makes a soft ball.

Bake in the oven for 30 minutes.

Cut into shapes and put the shapes on a baking tray.

Get these things: flour, butter, sugar.

Ask the children to cut out each of the instructions above and paste them back together in the correct order. They should then number the stages 1 to 6. Encourage them to keep reading through the instructions to check that they make sense.

From a Bean to a Bar   *(NLS: Y2 T1 T15)*